NEAR THE WINDOW TREE

poems and notes

by Karla Kuskin

HARPER & ROW, PUBLISHERS
New York, Evanston, San Francisco, London

NEAR THE WINDOW TREE
Copyright © 1975 by Karla Kuskin

Library of Congress Catalog Card Number: 74–20394
Trade Standard Book Number: 06–023539–X
Harpercrest Standard Book Number: 06–023540–3
FIRST EDITION

For Rose and Ace
(wherever they are)

CHILDREN MAY SKIP THIS INTRODUCTION

Where do you get the idea for a poem? . . .
Does it shake you awake?
Do you dream it asleep?
. . . [Does it] pop from your pen
When you are not aware
Or leap from your pocket
Or fall from your hair
Or is it just silently
Suddenly
There?

The question at hand is spoken in the first line of the verse above. Read your work to children and they will ask, "Where do you get your ideas?" That is what I have tried to answer here. There are 32 verses in this book. Many of them are preceded by a short paragraph which tells as simply as possible where a particular verse began: with a mood, a memory, a purr, a persistent image. Anywhere. Everywhere.

In addition to their individual beginnings these poems, like all poetry, have a collective birthplace: the interior of an author's head.

Encourage children to read and write poetry and they will be encouraged to reach into themselves and articulate feelings and dreams. Clearly a good science report and a good poem are not created by the same process. And yet it is common to judge children's accomplishments only in terms of action and concrete production. The notes and study that go into the science report are easy to appreciate, but daydreaming and reflection, those silent pursuits that lead one inside oneself, are generally dismissed as inaction and therefore a waste of time. The imagination is a temperamental beast. Shy of groups and timetables, it thrives on solitude and freedom.

Too often a fence of formality is built around the idea of "poetry" early in our lives. The very young have an easy affinity for rhythm and the sounds of words. This can be smothered by emphasizing complex rules and unfamiliar subject matter instead of stressing familiar speech and humor, the simplicity and lyric quality of so much verse. Make poetry accessible to children and they will have a form of self-expression as satisfying as singing or shouting.

A Frenchman, Joseph Joubert, once said, "You will find poetry nowhere unless you bring some of it with you." But bring some with you and you will find it everywhere.

Karla Kuskin

NEAR
THE
WINDOW TREE

An Ursula Nordstrom Book

This is a picture that I drew of myself sitting in the red chair next to the bedroom window. The chair and the window look like themselves, but I'm not sure I did me very well. This room is on the fourth floor of a brick house in the city. From it I see a piece of grey wall, a piece of sky and the top of an ailanthus tree. In the summer I can see only leaves. At night a few stars blink through black leaves. The napping cat is Rosalie. She spends her days sleeping on my papers. She spends her nights singing and dancing. There are many places where I feel like a stranger. But I always feel at home here in my own place.

Three wishes
Three.
The first
A tree:
Dark bark
Green leaves
Under a bit of blue
A canopy
To glimpse sky through
To watch sun sift through
To catch light rain
Upon the leaves
And let it fall again.
A place to put my eye
Beyond the window frame.

Wish two:
A chair
Not hard or high
One that fits comfortably
Set by the window tree
An island in the room
For me
My own
Place to sit and be
Alone.

My tree
There.
Here my chair,
Me,
Rain, sky, sun.
All my wishes
All the things I need
But one
Wish three:
A book to read.

When I go to schools I read the stories and poems I write to the children there. And I draw. There are a lot of questions: "Can you draw King Kong?" "Can you draw me?" "Where do you get your ideas?" I am always asked that and it's hard to answer. Ideas come from seeing and feeling and remembering. They are everywhere around us like the air. Try to answer the question yourself when you draw a picture or write. Why did you draw that? Where do you think your idea began? Sometimes I know but at other times a group of words just settles in my head muttering. I don't know where they come from. But I am sure they will hang around in my mind until I try to make something out of them.

Where do you get the idea for a poem?
Pippety
Poppety
Peep.
Does it shake you awake?
Do you dream it asleep?
Or into your tiny tin head does it creep
And pop from your pen when you are not aware
Or leap from your pocket
Or fall from your hair
Or is it just silently
Suddenly
There?
In a beat
In a breath
In a pause
In a cry
One unblinking eye
That stares from the dark
That is deep in your head
Demanding attention
Until it is written
Until it is rotten
Until it is anything else but forgotten
Until it is read.

There are those days when it is damp and cold and grey. Then everything is the same grey color: the sky, the tree, the wall at the end of the yard. I feel that same grey feeling inside of me.

You can write about anything. You can write about things or feelings. When I have feelings that make me sad or angry I try to write them down to get them outside myself.

It is grey out.
It is grey in.
In me
It is as grey as the day is grey.
The trees look sad
And I,
Not knowing why I do,
Cry.

After the grey morning the wind began to blow. It blew harder and harder. It shook the door to the porch and the window. The tree swayed and the whole house trembled. The wind seemed to take hold of everything. It scattered newspapers and pushed people down the street. With those sounds in my head I daydreamed that the wind picked up a child and carried her off.

Days that the wind takes over
Blowing through the gardens
Blowing birds out of the street trees
Blowing cats around corners
Blowing my hair out
Blowing my heart apart
Blowing high in my head
Like the sea sound caught in a shell.
One child put her thin arms around the wind
And they went off together.
Later the wind came back
Alone.

Daydreaming. Try some. Sit very still in a quiet spot and let your mind go anywhere. Let your thoughts jump from place to place and follow them. Write them down.

I was coming home from Philadelphia on the train very late one night. As the train crossed over a river I looked down and saw the moon's reflection. I was very tired, almost asleep, and some sleepy rhymes went through my head. They woke me up a little and I wrote them down.

Moon
Have you met my mother?
Asleep in a chair there
Falling down hair.

Moon in the sky
Moon in the water
Have you met one another?
Moon face to moon face
Deep in that dark place
Suddenly bright.

Moon
Have you met my friend the night?

Some feelings stay the same no matter how old you get or how much you change. Until I was nearly through high school I was very small. I looked younger than all my friends. I'm an ordinary-sized adult now, but that feeling of being smaller comes back at times and I still don't like it.

Okay everybody, listen to this:
I am tired of being smaller
Than you
And them
And him
And trees and buildings.
So watch out
All you gorillas and adults
Beginning tomorrow morning
Boy
Am I going to be taller.

Nicholas has just come home from school. He storms upstairs, throws his books here, his sweatshirt there, has milk and Oreos. I am his mother. You know the way mothers talk. I ask him where he's been and what he's done. There are times when he just doesn't feel like saying much.

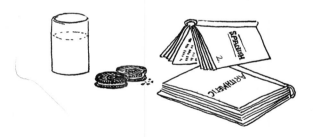

Where
Have you been dear?
What
Have you seen dear?
What
Did you do there?
Who
Went with you there?
Tell me
What's new dear?
What's
New with you dear?
Where
Will you go next?
What
Will you do?

"I do this and I do that.
I go here and I go there.
At times I like to be alone.
There are some thoughts that are my own
I do not wish to share."

Julia is nine. She can do back flips and handstands and somersaults. She's excellent at all of those but it scares me sometimes. I'm afraid she'll fall and really klunk herself.

I have a friend who keeps on standing on her hands.
That's fine,
Except I find it very difficult to talk to her
Unless I stand on mine.

Julia loves the color pink. Nicholas thinks it's terrible. What do you think...about pink? Jool has a pink checked cover on her bed. On top of that there are some dolls and pillows and her Koala bear. That is her favorite toy. Jool's father is a musician. He travels around a lot. He bought the Koala bear in Texas. I have to fix it now because one of its paws has fallen off. I think it has been hugged too much.

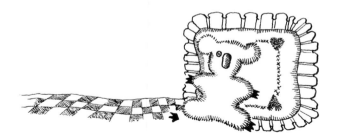

Koala means the world to her.
His nose and paws are getting bald.
Koala, whispered in his ear,
Is the only name he's called.
I cannot guess why he's preferred
To all the others sitting by—
The pandas, teddies, foreign dolls.
Koala has a missing eye.
He's made of fur.
Perhaps because he is so soft
She keeps him near.
There is a secret that she sees
That I don't see in him
That's clear.
Koala means the world to her.

Julia is in her room sitting next to Koala doing math. She doesn't like it at all. She would rather be roller skating. I know you. You'd rather do multiplication, right?

Is six times one a lot of fun?
Or eight times two?
Perhaps for you.
But five times three
Unhinges me,
While six and seven and eight times eight
Put me in an awful state
And four and six and nine times nine
Make me want to cry and whine
So when I get to twelve times ten
I begin to wonder when
I can take a vacation from multiplication
And go out
And start playing again.

There is a paperweight on the shelf. I bought it for Julia two Christmases ago. It is a round glass ball and inside it there are an evergreen tree, a house and a tiny snowman. When you pick up the paperweight and turn it upside down, snow rushes all around, making a small storm. Imagine being in there.

A tiny house,
A Christmas tree
Within a round glass globe
And me.
The house is cookie color brown,
The tree: deep green,
And I am so
Amazed to see us upside down
And covered suddenly with snow.

When I was nine we spent a month in the country. There were woods behind the house. One day I got very mad at my mother. I decided to run away from home. I packed everything I needed: the book I was reading and candy. I was going to stay away until they were really scared, maybe a week. The sun was hot and bright but as I entered the woods the trees blocked it out. It was cool and dark. Suddenly there was a very large spider web right in front of me. There was a very large spider in it. I've always been afraid of spiders so I went home.

Running away
From the rest of today
Running away
From you
Running away
From "Don't do that"
From all of the things
I must constantly do.
I feel too tall
I feel too old
For a hundred helpings of being told.
Packing my head
Taking my feet
Galloping down the familiar street.
My head is a bird.
My heart is free again.
I might come back
When I feel like me again.

Sometimes, holding my red pen in my hand, I look at the blank paper in front of me and my head seems as blank as the paper. It seems as empty as a cookie jar with no cookies in it. Like a gum machine with no gum. Not one idea in there...just air. One day I began to think of all the things people always write about. The same things over and over—dove, love, moon, June. Then I decided to try and find a subject no one ever writes about. I had never read a poem about a radish so I thought I would write one. But when I got near the end of my poem, the radish turned into the moon. I really don't know how that happened. Have you ever tried to write about something unusual like an armadillo or a pickle?

Write about a radish
Too many people write about the moon.

The night is black
The stars are small and high
The clock unwinds its ever-ticking tune
Hills gleam dimly
Distant nighthawks cry.
A radish rises in the waiting sky.

35

Once in a while I look out at the tree in the yard. Then I look at the blank paper on my lap and I try to get the tree to give me an idea for something to write about.

Tree birds
Light like leaves
On trees.
Twitter,
Glitter,
Ease into a passing breeze
And leave for greener trees.

Listen to the sound of words. There are light sounds and heavy ones. "Whippoorwill" has a musical sound. "Belch" sounds short and squat like a toad.

When you say the same word over and over, you forget the meaning and it begins to sound very funny: spaghetti, spaghetti, spaghetti, spaghetti, spaghetti, spaghetti, spaghetti, spaghetti, spa-ghet-ti . . . spaghetti.

"Cow" sounds heavy.
Cow
Standing in the meadow
Chewing.
A big fur box on legs
Mooing.

Some words look and sound like their meaning:

hop

hop   *hop,*

        hop

                      hop

or elephant; anything called an **ELEPHANT**
must be enormous.

Worm

Is a term for a worm.
It sounds like a worm looks
Slow
Low to the ground
Usually brown
It would never have feathers
It would not sing at all
With a name like worm
It must be long and thin
And crawl.

Once I wrote a poem that goes like this:
I like bugs.
I kiss them
And I give them hugs.

When I read it in schools the children laugh a little. Some say "Yuck" or "Ugh." Bug is such a short, funny word that I decided to write some more bug poems. They are like the word "bug": pretty silly.

Bug
Met a dragon
In the park.
La la.
The moon was down
The night was dark.
La la.
The dragon opened up his mouth
And fearful flames frothed north by south
And west by east.
The bug deceased.
La la.

Bugs never speak.
I wonder why?
Perhaps they're shy.

Many people who are smart
In physics, French and math and art
Cannot tell two bugs apart.

Bugs are just not very smart
In math or physics, French or art.
But *they* can tell two bugs apart.

Buggity
Buggity
Bug
Wandering aimlessly
Buggishly smug
When all of a sudden along came a shoe
Out with another shoe
Wandering too.
The shoes went on wandering:
Left,
Right,
Left,
Splat.

Bugs
Very frequently perish like that.

A bug sat in a silver flower
Thinking silver thoughts.
A bigger bug out for a walk
Climbed up that silver flower stalk
And snapped the small bug down his jaws
Without a pause
Without a care
For all the bug's small silver thoughts.
It isn't right
It isn't fair
That big bug ate that little bug
Because that little bug was there.

He also ate his underwear.

We have a cat named Rosalie Katskin. She is black and beautiful and big. I read somewhere that cats, like lions and tigers, sleep twenty hours every day. Rose sleeps wherever I'm working. She especially likes to curl up in the middle of the papers I am working on. When she finally wakes up at four in the morning, she zooms around bumping into walls and dashing through doors like a racing car gone crazy.

Julia loves her Rosalie.
Rosalie the cat.
Julia pets her nosealie.
Soft, disdainful Rosalie.
Steps upon her toesalie
Pulls her tail and
Ohsalie
Julia has a scratch.

While Rosalie guileless
And practically smileless
Suns quietly, sly on her mat.

In addition to Rosalie we have had two other cats: Ace and Charlotte. I have watched them day after day and they are always changing. Writing about them is like trying to sketch with words. I want to catch what I see when a cat is sleeping or running wild or walking or stretching or teasing Jool. These poems are quick pictures of Rose, Acey and Char.

The terrible cat of black velvet fur
Will leap at your legs
with a thunderous purrrr
Flash through the air
To a lap
Or a chair
Nibble your dinner
And probably stare
At your face and your frown
As she daintily tears
The chop you were eating
And swallows it down.

That cat is crazy
Just a bit
Elegant
Mysterious
Dancing on the midnight grasses
Moonlit
Very royal
Delirious.

When a cat is asleep
There is nothing asleep
That is quite so asleep
As a cat.

She has finished with darting,
Careening and leaping
Now even the soft air around her is sleeping.

Take a word like cat
And build around it;
A fur room over here
A long meow
Floating from the chimney like a smoke tail.
Draw with words.
Balance them like blocks.
Carve word furniture:
A jar of pussy willows,
Catkins, phlox,
Milk in a dish,
Catnip pillows,
A silver bell,
A plaster bird,
An eaten fish.
When everything is perfect in its place
Step back to view the home
That you have built of words around your word.
It is a poem.

This cat
Walks into the room and across the floor,
Under a chair, around the bed,
Behind the table and out the door.
I'm sitting on the chair
And I don't see where he is.
I don't see one hair of his.
I just hear the floorboards scarcely squeak.
This cat comes and goes
On invisible toes.
The sneak.

Examining the breeze.
A package neatly wrapped with tail
Flicks a whisker
Pleased.

Upon the stair.
Taking the air.
Unquestioned owner
Of the comfortable chair.

Napping everywhere
Stretched in the sun
As if the sun were hers
Awash in warmth
And furs.

The flow of a cat walking
Over the lawn
To place herself like a soft stone
In the middle of the paper
I am working on.

I do not wish I were a cat
With fine black whiskers
Smoky fur.
I do not want a tail and paws
I only wish that I could purr.

Julia has a new blue raincoat with a hood. Nicholas' jacket has a hood. My coat has a hood. I love it. I go out for a walk and I begin to feel cold so I put up my hood and I'm warm. If it begins to rain I put up my hood and I'm dry. It doesn't matter if I don't have a hat or an umbrella. Rosalie is the only one without a hood. How would a cat look with a hood on?

The house of snail upon his back
Protects from weather and attack
Though just who might attack a snail
Is a question I must fail to answer.

The turtle in his turtle shell
Is shell-tered well.
The only skin that shows a bit
On him
Is nose and toes a bit
On him.

I have a blue coat with a hood
Like a private tent or roof
Water, every weather proof.
Warm, secure
A snuggery
It often walks around with me.
A home away when I'm away
Letting all the stars in
Keeping out the damp grey
True
Good
Blue
Hood
It suits me well
My shell.

Coming home one night in the car I kept seeing men with mustaches. All the mustaches looked alike. So did all the men. And this verse went through my head over and over, with the end running back to the beginning like a dog chasing its tail.

The streets are filled with mustached men
Looking like each other
Who?
The streets
Are filled with mustached men
Looking like each other
Who?
The
Streets
Are filled with mustached men
Looking like each other
Who?
The streets are
Filled
With mustached men
Looking like each other
Who?

The summer I was six I went to camp in the country. I only felt homesick at the end of the day. It's a nice time but a sad one. Maybe because it is the end. It has a special color too. When you were younger did you have to go to bed when it was still light out? Julia would say "It isn't fair." That's the way I felt then. All those voices playing in the street, while I lay there, wide awake, in bed.

This poem is almost like a song. Maybe a lullaby. I wish you would make up a tune to go with it.

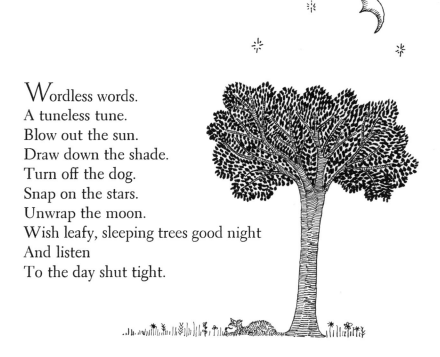

Wordless words.
A tuneless tune.
Blow out the sun.
Draw down the shade.
Turn off the dog.
Snap on the stars.
Unwrap the moon.
Wish leafy, sleeping trees good night
And listen
To the day shut tight.